A GLORY IS A GROUP OF ANGELS, A GATHERING, A BAND.
There is such a band in a mosaic built into the chancel wall of
Memorial Church. Maurizio Camerino of A. Salviati & Co.,
the firm in Venice, Italy, that made all the church mosaics once
wrote: "With the sketch . . . of the *Glory of the Angels,* I went to
see Mrs. Stanford again. She was greatly pleased." Many gen-
erations since Jane Stanford have been "greatly pleased" with
this glory and with the other glories that contribute to this
American Renaissance masterpiece. We invite you to join them.

Editor: Raymond Hardie
Production Manager: Nora Sweeny
Designer: Paul Carstensen

Our grateful thanks to Edie F. Barry and Bruce Anderson
of the Stanford Alumni Association; to Imelda White and
Judy Werner-Hall at Stanford Memorial Church; Margaret
Kimball, Linda Long and Tim Noakes at the Stanford
University Archives; Joseph A. Taylor at the Tile Heritage
Foundation; and McKernan Satterlee Associates, Inc.

PHOTO CREDITS: All photographs in this book were taken
by Richard Barnes except the following: Bruce Shippee
courtesy of the Tile Heritage Foundation: pages 4-5, 37,
48-49, 52, 59, 64; McKernan Satterlee Associates: page 60;
Department of Special Collections, Stanford University
Archives: pages 15, 16, 17, 20-21, 24, 27, 28.

Reproduction of the painting on page 54 by permission
of the Birmingham Museums and Art Gallery.

ISBN # 0916318-54-0

ROBERT C. GREGG ▪ KAREN BARTHOLOMEW ▪ LESLEY BONE

Principal photography by RICHARD BARNES

Stanford Memorial Church
GLORY *of* ANGELS

STANFORD ALUMNI ASSOCIATION ▪ STANFORD, CALIFORNIA

CONTENTS

GLORY

I N THE PAGES THAT FOLLOW, YOU will be treated to images and text that tell you much about the history, design and decoration of Stanford Memorial Church. The building is unusual. Physically, as a university chapel, the church surprises, since it is of cathedral proportions, splendid in its stone, mosaic and stained-glass artistry. Pipe organs in Memorial Church are of superior quality, making this sanctuary one of California's premier venues for instrumental and choral performance. As a grand piece of architecture, Stanford Memorial

Previous page: This is one of the large mosaic pendentive angels, also shown on pages 32 and 56. (Dome, atop one of the four pillars)

Church draws visitors from near and far.

The uses of the church may also surprise —the building seems rarely to be empty. A number of services take place in a normal week, serving the needs of several Protestant Christian gatherings as well as the Roman Catholic community. Weddings are celebrated on Saturdays and Sundays. Memorial tributes or funeral services are frequently held, either in the main church or in the side chapel. Visitors often find music rehearsals or performances under way. In addition, for many of its hours, Memorial Church fulfills one of the chief wishes of its founders: People in the surrounding community, Stanford students, staff members and faculty, as well as patients in the medical center and their families, come to the sanctuary for quiet, for reflection and for private devotions.

Both newcomers and longtime residents sometimes ask, "What kind of religious building is Memorial Church?" First, it is decidedly a Christian building, as its shape, symbols, artwork and usual forms of worship make apparent. The Stanfords built the church with the understanding that "moral and spiritual instruction . . . important to the young men and women who come here" would emanate from the church and be heard from its pulpit. Their assumptions about the content of that instruction were those of late 19th-century liberal Protestants (as the inscriptions within the church reveal), but they explicitly urged that teachers from the great religions of the world be invited to speak in this University chapel. Stipulating

Memorial Church is a work meant to glorify God and to fix in memory those named in its dedications.

The Stanfords sought to protect free intellectual inquiry— in classroom, laboratory and church.

that Memorial Church, like the University itself, would remain "nonsectarian" (that is, not affiliated with any one Protestant denomination), the Stanfords sought to protect free intellectual inquiry—in classroom, laboratory and church—from any interference prompted by the caution or dogmatism of religious authorities.

CONVINCED, LIKE MANY OF THEIR CONtemporaries, that religious life consisted primarily in individuals' considerations of moral and spiritual ideals, Leland and Jane Stanford could not have foreseen that time would bring other understandings of religion to the fore —most notably, a sense of religious quest and relationship to God that unfolds within a distinct faith community. Indeed, the founders

did not anticipate the presence on campus of Jewish, Muslim, Buddhist, Hindu and Baha'i communities. Because of its iconography, Memorial Church is not well suited to the worship and assembly needs of those religious groups, and therefore other places of congregation are now being planned. Today, those who assemble for worship at Memorial Church are, for the most part, members of identifiable Christian traditions, even if they can only be "denominated" as ecumenical Protestant or Roman Catholic Christians.

A jewel of many facets, Memorial Church appeals to worshippers who regularly gather there, to those who have made this sanctuary their place of meditation, and to numerous lovers of music, art and architecture. The grandeur of the church, articulated in its details, greatly occupied Jane Stanford—the structure was to be without flaw. Memorial Church is a work meant to glorify God and to fix in memory those named in its dedications. At least two other "messages" were intended by the building and what transpires in it.

One was clearly in the form of an exhortation and was presented early to the faculty and administrators in blunt (and perhaps overconfident) terms: "The church is the only institution that makes or has made or pretends to make a stand against immorality in all its forms. Education does not; nor does that science in which you are interested and which you consider all powerful." Jane Stanford's concern had to do with the school's ethos, convinced as she was that learning, without attention to character, would not benefit those who came to study and prepare for their lives of usefulness.

Another message more poignant and personal to the Stanfords is impossible to miss in Memorial Church: Statements of the founders' own experiences and realizations are visible in the cruciform interior, in the image in the west arcade of the young boy being lifted to heaven by angels, and in the prominent inscription beneath the angel lectern about the meeting of human and divine life in suffering. To the realities of brokenness, recovery and hope, the Stanfords were no strangers. Memorial Church was built to honor the God in whom they found strength and continues to welcome and encourage all in similar need.

To the realities of brokenness, recovery and hope, the Stanfords were no strangers.

PAST
GLORY

MEMORIAL CHURCH STANDS at the very heart of the Stanford campus. It is the focal point of the Main Quadrangle—the principal building that is seen as the visitor approaches the University along Palm Drive from Palo Alto. With its extensive mosaics, stained glass windows and stone carvings, Memorial Church is one of Stanford's architectural gems. ⚘ Leland and Jane Lathrop Stanford founded the University as a memorial to their only child, Leland Stanford Jr., who died of typhoid fever at age 15.

Previous page: The Murray-Harris organ stands to the left. The mosaic God Separating Darkness from Light *is on the wall of the east nave. (East organ loft)*

This photo of the church, taken before the 1906 earthquake, shows the 80-foot tower that had a clock face on four sides.

The central location of the church indicates the importance that the founders placed on the church's role in the lives of the students. Even so, Leland and Jane Stanford specified that attendance by students would be voluntary and that the church would be nondenominational. In his address at the University's opening on October 1, 1891, Senator Leland Stanford said that he and his wife expected the students to graduate "with a lofty sense of man's and woman's responsibilities on earth in accordance with the highest teachings of morality and religion."

FROM THE BEGINNING, JANE LATHROP Stanford took special interest in two large projects—the museum and the church. The museum was her personal memorial to her son, and the church her memorial to her husband, who died in 1893, two years after the University opened. His death left the University in financial turmoil for years while legal disputes tied up the Stanford estate. In 1898, the legal issues were settled in Jane Stanford's favor, and she proceeded with long-delayed plans to complete construction of the University, including Memorial Church.

With the death of her husband, Jane Stanford transformed herself from a retiring woman into a determined University administrator and trustee. She always saw the church as a force in University life. "While my whole heart is in the University," she told Professor John Casper Branner, who later became the University's second president, "my soul is in that church."

A deeply religious woman, Jane Stanford attended various Protestant churches but was also attracted to the ritual and tradition of Catholicism, of which some influences can be seen in the church. Like her husband, however, she never espoused any particular denomination.

MEMORIAL CHURCH IS A CRUCIFORM-style building, with the transept intersecting the nave-chancel axis at the crossing, which is marked by four arches and a dome. The original 1887 architectural design of the building was the work of Charles Coolidge of Boston. Coolidge based his mixture of Romanesque and Mission Revival design for both the Quadrangle and the church on the work of his mentor, the highly respected H. H.

The Stanfords with their only son, Leland Jr. The photograph was taken in Paris around 1881.

The chancel of the pre-1906 church had large marble statues of the apostles placed around the altar. These were originally intended to stand in the golden niches in the wall but, on delivery, were found to be too large.

Richardson. Richardson Romanesque is marked by rough-hewn stonework, low arches, round turrets, tile roofs and stone carving accents. Memorial Church was loosely modeled after Richardson's Trinity Church in Boston. Reminiscent of Europe's early Romanesque churches in its outline, curvature and bulk, Memorial Church is a Victorian interpretation constructed for American tastes.

After completing the Inner Quadrangle, Coolidge's firm withdrew from the campus project, and in 1898 Jane Stanford hired San Francisco architect Clinton Day to finish Coolidge's work.

It was Jane Stanford's idea—considered idiosyncratic by some architectural historians —to add extensive mosaics to the building's façade and interior. During her travels in Europe, she and Senator Stanford had admired mosaic decoration. While in Venice, they became friends with Maurizio Camerino of A. Salviati & Co., then undertaking the renovation of the exquisite mosaics in Venice's San Marco Cathedral. The Stanfords asked Camerino to come to Florence to assist them when Leland Jr. died there in 1884.

Most of the designs for the Stanford murals were based on scenes from the Old Testament and were created by Salviati's chief designer, Antonio Paoletti. The exception is the façade mosaic. In a contract signed in December 1900, this mural was described as a "big picture on the gable outside the church . . . representing 'Christ blessing the people.'" Sometime in the next decade, the mural became popularly known as *The Sermon on*

This window, The Annunciation, *was based on a watercolor by the Pre-Raphaelite Frederick James Shields. Like the chandelier in the foreground, it shows a definite Art Nouveau influence. (Wall of the east nave)*

the Mount. Almost certainly this mosaic does not represent that scene, which refers to a series of teachings delivered in the hill country of Galilee (Matthew 5:1-7:29) and which depicts Jesus seated. The biblical reference most consistent with *Christ Blessing the People,* the title used in 1900 by Camerino, is Luke 24:50-51. This describes Jesus after the Resurrection. "Then he led them out as far as Bethany, and lifting up his hands, he blessed them. While he was blessing them, he withdrew from them and was carried up into heaven." This is the only reference in the Bible to Jesus lifting his hands in this way.

MEMORIAL CHURCH'S LARGE STAINED glass windows are based on paintings of New Testament stories. Jane Stanford selected

these particular works from books of religious art and even from postcards she collected. She selected J. & R. Lamb Studios of New York City to translate the paintings into glass and, all told, the chief designer, Frederick Stymetz Lamb, constructed and installed 140 windows. Jane Stanford chose Lamb, a master craftsman, because he showed strong interest in the ecclesiastical rather than commercial aspect of the work and he took the time to explain the stained glass process. Trained as a painter, Lamb studied under Sir John Everett Millais in Paris. He was also an expert in glass chemistry and had a thorough understanding of the techniques of stained glass construction. Lamb won gold medals from the French government and in the 1895 Atlanta Exposition and earned an honorable mention at the

The pre-1906 campus is seen from the other side of Lake Lagunita. The memorial arch (left of the church), the 80-foot tower of the church and the furnace chimney (right) all collapsed during the earthquake.

1893 Chicago Exposition. The Stanford commission was one of the largest awarded to an American stained glass artist up to that time. Today, the Stanford stained glass windows are considered the finest example of Frederick Lamb's work.

⚜

GROUND FOR THE CHURCH WAS BROKEN in May 1899, and construction began in earnest following a simple ceremony on January 29, 1900, during which Jane Stanford placed mementos and various documents in a cornerstone.

The sandstone used in the construction of the church came from the Goodrich quarry in the Almaden area of San Jose and was brought to the University by rail. It was first rough-cut in the Quad and then installed in the church. The quality of the stonework is due, in great part, to the skill and exacting nature of John D. McGilvray, who also supervised the construction of many other campus buildings.

Jane Stanford was involved in every part of the process. Resident architect Charles Hodges recalled that she could read blueprints like an expert, and she would follow him to the high scaffolding holding onto his coat. He said that Jane Stanford "invariably carried a parasol. It was notched at the lower end. She would run it into the carving and, if it did not come up to the mark, she would ask me to have it cut a little deeper."

Jane Stanford kept in mind the depth of those carvings in medieval churches she had admired and was determined that Memorial

A section of The Glory of Angels *is shown beneath a mosaic band of* The Prophets. *Jane Stanford insisted on the depth of the stone carvings on the capitals (foreground). Each cherubic face was unique, and the children living on campus at the time are said to have served as models. (Chancel)*

Church should equal them in quality of workmanship. She also made note of inspirational sayings she came upon, and later adapted and combined them for workmen to carve in the church walls. The few inscriptions in quotations are taken from the Bible.

Although the church was completed and dedicated in 1903, decorative work continued for another two years. Installation of mosaics and carving of quotations on interior walls proceeded simultaneously, with workers climbing high scaffolding above the pews and up into the four central arches.

THE CHURCH WAS DEDICATED ON JANUARY 25, 1903. Bertha Berner, Jane Stanford's companion and secretary, later wrote that "words fail in expressing the satisfaction experienced

The façade of the pre-1906 church shows the original rose window, with the face of a small child at the center. The two figures at either side of the large mosaic were later removed and the bottom portion redesigned.

by [Jane] Stanford on reaching this crowning point in her life." A little more than two years later, on February 28, 1905, Jane Stanford died in Honolulu, just a few months before final touches were applied to her beloved church. She was therefore spared the agony of seeing the church, the museum and many other campus buildings severely damaged on April 18, 1906, when a severe earthquake struck the San Francisco Bay Area. The quake badly damaged or destroyed many of the larger, more ornate buildings, while the older, lower and more structurally sound Quadrangle buildings suffered relatively less.

During the church construction, the crossing structure had not been adequately connected to the roofs and walls around it. When the ground started shaking, the crossing smashed against the roofs over the nave, chancel and the east and west transepts, ripping open huge holes.

An 80-foot-high, 12-sided spire sat atop the crossing structure. It had two rows of large stained glass windows and contained a clock with chimes. From the inside, pre-earthquake churchgoers who looked up into the tower's dome saw a frescoed Victorian interpretation of God's Eye—complete with tear—surrounded by cherubs and a shooting star.

During the earthquake, the tower and its Eye dropped onto the chancel roof, spreading debris everywhere. There were 12 marble statues of the apostles placed in front of the niches around the altar, and many of these were severely damaged. Meanwhile, as the nave roof bounced about, its weak connection to the front mosaic-covered façade gave way, and the front wall fell forward into the Inner Quad courtyard. The four soaring angels placed up in the crossing were the only major mosaics spared destruction. Workers dismantled the church stone by stone, leaving in place the crossing structure and church offices, known as the Round Room. Stones and stained glass windows were labeled and stored for future use.

Two years after the 1906 quake, which was later estimated to have been 8.3 on the Richter scale, reconstruction began with a firm intention to protect the building from future earthquakes.

For the second construction of the church, stones were anchored to thick, concrete-reinforced walls. Artisans from Salviati & Co. returned in early 1914 to install new mosaics, including a redesigned mural for the front.

Originally, a gigantic inscription on the façade read: "Memorial Church. Erected to the glory of God and in loving memory of my husband Leland Stanford." In the reconstruction, University trustees relocated the inscription and added Jane Stanford's name to a much smaller dedicatory plaque placed at the lower left of the façade, a move the alumni magazine labeled "a tremendous improvement." This left the question of what to put in the large blank space. Camerino offered (free of charge and using mosaics on hand) to provide some general background, consisting of "pools of water surrounded by tropical plants and lilies." Within months of completion of the façade mosaic in October 1914, trustees were dissatisfied with the effect and decided to make yet another change. John K. Branner, an architect and son of University President John Casper Branner, suggested the simplified revision that can be seen today. With work on the interior mosaics finally complete, the *Stanford Alumnus* in January 1917 reported that "the church, for almost the first time since it was begun, is finished."

University trustees replaced Lamb's original rose window with a simple arched window they thought would be more in harmony with the mission style of the Quadrangle. They also replaced the tile floor with cork.

The trustees initially were undecided

The church was very badly damaged by the 1906 earthquake. The 80-foot tower collapsed, causing the façade to be blown out. The whole church was dismantled, and each stone was numbered in preparation for rebuilding. In the reconstruction, the gigantic inscription was replaced by a smaller dedicatory plaque placed at the lower left of the façade, and Jane Stanford's name was added.

about rebuilding the tower. Within two weeks of the earthquake, newspapers were reporting it would not be rebuilt; but five years later, trustees did in fact study possible designs for a new tower. In the end, they could not agree on its design and eventually decided to leave the task to a future generation. They finished the base of the tower with a tile roof and exterior skylight. Inside, in place of God's Eye, they installed a dome topped by a simple skylight and frescoed ceiling with designs in bronze rather than the gold leaf that was used on the sides of the drum.

IN ADDITION TO PROVIDING THE SETTING for regular worship, Memorial Church has been used through the years for numerous weddings, infant baptisms, memorial services (including Jane Stanford's), musical performances and a variety of other events, such as the 1994 visit by the Dalai Lama. During the late 1960s and early 1970s, students crowded into the church to hear antiwar speeches by such notables as Nobel laureate Linus Pauling and religious leaders William Sloan Coffin, Robert McAfee Brown and B. Davie Napier, who served as dean of the chapel.

More than 7,000 couples have been united in Memorial Church since the first bride and groom, William A. and Ethel Rhodes Holt, both members of the Class of 1902, were married on February 22, 1903. The church now hosts about 150 weddings a year.

ON OCTOBER 17, 1989, THE UNIVERSITY was rocked again by an earthquake. The Loma

God's Eye, which was painted on the inside of the dome of the pre-1906 church, is realistically represented with a large tear about to fall. Cherubs peep out from behind the clouds, stars adorn the sky, and a prophetic shooting star trails down one side. The frescoed ceilings were colored in rich reds and blues.

Prieta quake damaged the crossing structure, the major component of the present church that was not dismantled and rebuilt in 1913.

When the earthquake hit, the crossing structure flexed, causing several stones in the north and west arches to slip as much as 2 inches. In the northeast corner, an 8-foot section of mosaic from the angel's left wing broke away and crashed 70 feet to the floor. Several stones from the east arch wall slipped, and some of these facing stones fell onto pews in the balconies. The organ-loft railing collapsed inward.

Though the visible damage this time was relatively modest, the church was closed, and plans to repair the building and brace it against future major quakes were started. Former University trustee Melvin B. Lane

led a $10 million fund-raising drive for the project, with $1.5 million set aside as an endowed maintenance fund.

This time, to strengthen the crossing structure, engineers used 469 tons of concrete and 22 tons of steel, in an innovative, hidden technique, to brace the structure behind the dome and secure the whole crossing to the rest of the building.

The 1913 roofs were rebuilt with plywood diaphragms, over which 30,000 red clay tiles were reinstalled. The wing of the angel located in the northeast corner was restored. A new backing system was made to secure both this angel and the three other mosaic angels around the base of the dome to the building. Stones in the decorative arches were jacked back into position.

This small mosaic, Moses Saved from the Waters, *is framed by elaborately carved stone arches. The stones in the church were rough-cut in the Quad. After they had been installed, the fine detail was carved. The carvers had to present a clay model of each design for approval before they could proceed. A team of 10 men spent two years on scaffolds carving these stone arches and borders. (Above the west arcade)*

The Victorian chandeliers were repaired and rewired. The transept balconies, closed for two decades by the county fire marshal, were reopened with the addition of emergency exits. (The false doors on the south side of each balcony were transformed into real doors and connections made to existing staircases inside the building.)

The church was rededicated on November 1, 1992. Starting outside, the congregation heard brief remarks and joined in a responsive reading. Following the Christian tradition for opening of churches, Dean of the Chapel Robert C. Gregg knocked three times on the church's middle door, and the congregation followed him inside. In his remarks during the service, Dean Gregg proudly declared, "This splendid building revives."

PRESENT
GLORY

MEMORIAL CHURCH WAS built during the American Renaissance. This was a period of industrial expansion and massive population growth resulting in a surge in national confidence and optimism. The arts, from architecture to weaving, blossomed. American artists looked to the best traditions in Europe and melded them to create a unique late-Victorian style, which has come to be known as American Renaissance. Choosing the best from all cultures was seen as the way to create a great American civilization.

Previous page: This is one of the four angels in the pendentives, also shown on pages 6 and 56. There was an astonishing range of colors available to these mosaic craftsmen. Thirty-four different shades of pink were used to construct the area of the cheek below the eye. During the 1989 earthquake, an 8-foot section of the left wing of this angel crashed 70 feet to the floor of the crossing below. (Dome, atop supporting pillar)

One of the four intricately carved arches under the dome frames the organ loft with the Fisk-Nanney organ in the center, and the east nave with the Garden of Eden mural over the door. (Front doors of church from the chancel)

VANTAGE POINTS

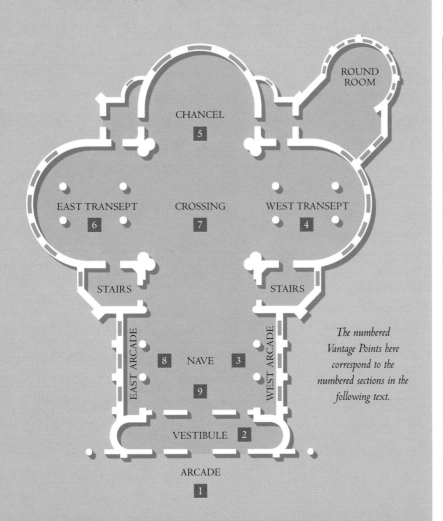

ROUND ROOM

CHANCEL

5

EAST TRANSEPT

6

CROSSING

7

WEST TRANSEPT

4

STAIRS

STAIRS

EAST ARCADE

WEST ARCADE

8   NAVE   3

9

The numbered Vantage Points here correspond to the numbered sections in the following text.

VESTIBULE   2

ARCADE

I

Memorial Church is a perfect example of this movement. There are traces of the great Italian Renaissance artists and the fine decorative influences of the medieval period, as well as works inspired by the Byzantine tradition. There are also strong influences from the Romanesque period and the more contemporary Pre-Raphaelites. Elements of all these styles can be found here.

⚜

I STARTING IN FRONT OF THE church, the visitor's eye is drawn upward to the simple Celtic cross that crowns the top of the façade. The three arms end in a trefoil shape, which is the emblem for the Trinity. This cross is a recurring symbol in the church. A new central shaft was added after the 1989 Loma Prieta earthquake, but the arms are part of the original, which was placed there during the reconstruction following the 1906 earthquake.

The extraordinary mosaic under the cross is *Christ Blessing the People*, based on the text from Luke 24:50. At the time it was completed, it was the largest mosaic ever installed in the United States. It is 30 feet high by 84 feet wide and represents the moment just before Christ's ascension into heaven. After Jane Stanford's death, this mosaic seems to have been misinterpreted as *The Sermon on the Mount*. A number of clues, however, point to it being the moment just before the ascension. A wound from the crucifixion is evident on Christ's upraised right hand and two Roman soldiers stand halfway up the right side of the scene. There are 51 characters, including Christ, and at Jane Stanford's insistence the scene included both men and women.

The large middle window was replaced after the 1906 earthquake. It is the only window that cannot be viewed from the inside because it is boxed in by the central organ. This window, known as *Lilies of the Field*, is shaped like an arch and was executed in the style of the early 1900s. There is a cross in the center made of faceted pieces of glass that are inset like gems. These "jewels" are meant to catch the light and sparkle. The smaller windows at either side are made of opalescent panels of glass and match the other nonpictorial windows inside.

In the lower mosaics, the Graces are shown intertwined in a vine that represents the "tree of life." Love is depicted in a charm-

This detail of God in the burning bush is taken from the mosaic Moses Ordered to Take Israel Out of Egypt, *which is beside the window* Lo, I Am with You Always. *The complete mosaic is shown on page 43. (West side of nave)*

ing tableau that shows a mother with wings surrounded by children.

⚜

2 THE DETAILS OF THE PILLAR carvings on the three arches and in the small decorative stone band above the lower mosaics show the variety of designs used by the stone carvers working on the church. No two pillars have the same motif because each carver used his own pattern.

Past the arches, in the arcade, there are three pairs of handsome cast bronze doors, each bearing one of the recurring Victorian themes in the church, the cherub.

Through the doors lies the vestibule. The contrast between the wall and floor mosaics is worthy of note. The marble floor tiles are larger and have a smoother surface than the

wall tiles. The floor mosaic shows a lamb surrounded by the symbols of the four evangelists: the winged angel (St. Matthew), the winged lion (St. Mark), the ox (St. Luke) and the eagle (St. John). Some of these symbols reappear in other areas of Memorial Church.

The mosaics on the walls of the church have been compared to a glittering tapestry. The shimmering quality of these mosaics was created by the use of different tones of gold and green. The alternating medallions represent the first and last letters of the Greek alphabet, Alpha and Omega. The other medallion, the Chi Rho, is Christ's monogram and combines the first two letters for "Christ" in the Greek alphabet. During the recent earthquake reconstruction, a piece of the original mosaic wall, with the Chi Rho from

Decorative mosaics cover the walls of the transepts. This design represents a sunburst, which is a symbol of Christ. The lunette, the semicircular space over the door, displays a group of Victorian cherubs. (West transept, exit door)

this area, was found in the foundation. The piece was incorporated into the Communion table that is used in the chancel and serves as a link with the pre-1906 church.

Once again, the representation of the Celtic cross is noteworthy in the stained glass above the central wooden door that leads into the nave. The Latin epigraph above the door on the left, *Domus Dei Locus Orationis*, translates as "The house of God, the place of prayer." The Latin epigraph above the door on the right, *Domus Dei Aula Coeli*, translates as "The house of God, the forecourt of heaven."

3. THE DOOR ON THE RIGHT LEADS into the west side of the nave of the church. Along this wall there is a series of

magnificent mosaics. From the back of the church these are: *Rebekah and Isaac, Rachel Sees Jacob Approaching, Moses Ordered to Take Israel Out of Egypt, Moses Sees the Promised Land* and *Joshua Finds a Captain for His Hosts*. There are also three large windows in this area. Both the windows and the mosaics have their biblical references below each scene.

The first window, *Lo, I Am with You Always*, was designed by Antonio Paoletti, the same artist who created the mosaics. He worked closely with Jane Stanford in the choice of subject for this window. On the far left, the figure of the dead boy is generally believed to represent the Stanfords' son, Leland Jr. The figure at the middle right is thought to be Leland Jr. being taken into heaven by angels.

The mosaic placed between this window

and the next depicts Moses stooping to remove his sandal. He is preparing to tread on sacred ground, while at the same time shielding his eyes from the blazing light of the Lord appearing above the burning bush.

Beside this mosaic is a window designed from a painting by the Norwegian artist Axel Ender and called *The Angel at the Tomb*. The white, opalescent glass used in the angel shows how Lamb created subtle shadows in the robe by placing layers of colored glass behind the white. The luminescent effect of the whole is dramatized by the dark background against which the angel is set.

The following window, *The Dream of Pilate's Wife*, is a favorite with stained glass historians because, up until that period, it was rare to find a woman as the main sub-ject. The design was taken from an etching by the French sculptor and illustrator Gustave Doré. The original was one of 250 etchings used to illustrate a two-volume Bible published in 1866. The milky-colored glass with violet streaks was one of Lamb's favorite choices for angel wings.

The clerestory windows, above the west arcade, represent single figures of saints, evangelists and angels. Starting from the right, they are: Hope, St. John, St. Priscilla, St. Peter, St. Agnes, St. Stephen and two angels. The central pair of windows almost have the quality of a watercolor. This effect is created by subtle color layerings and the mixing that take place when the light passes through those different layers. Unfortunately, the angel windows do not transmit any direct sunlight and

This window, Lo, I Am with You Always, *was designed by Antonio Paoletti, the designer of the mosaics. The figure of the dead boy and the figure being taken up into heaven by angels are generally believed to represent the Stanfords' son Leland Jr., shown in the family photograph on page 17. A detail of this window is shown on the cover of this book. The mosaic to the right is* Rachel Sees Jacob Approaching. *(West nave, first window)*

The window The Dream of Pilate's Wife *(left) is based on an illustration by the French artist Gustave Doré. The mosaic (right) is* Moses Sees the Promised Land. *The window* The Angel at the Tomb *(center) is based on a painting by the Norwegian artist Axel Ender. The next mosaic is* Moses Ordered to Take Israel Out of Egypt, *details of which can be seen on pages 37 and 52. (West nave)*

so appear lifeless. The contrast emphasizes the major role that light plays in this art form. The mosaics between these windows, starting from the right, are: *The Sale of Joseph, Jacob Going to Canaan, Isaac Blessing Jacob, The Dream of Jacob* and *Abraham Restrained from Offering Up Isaac.*

Below these windows are wonderful mosaic vignettes. Starting from the right they represent: *Moses Receiving the Tablets of Law, Joshua Successor of Moses, David Anointed for the First Time, The Meeting of David with Abigail* and *David Singing Psalms.*

The clerestory windows and the mosaics above the east arcade are best viewed from this point. (Information about these is provided in Vantage Point 8.)

Around the corner, there is a large mural above the west transept door. This represents *Predictions of the Prophets Concerning the Coming of the Lord.* Its cold gray and blue tones are in sharp contrast to the mural facing it, the *Garden of Eden,* which has a multitude of warm green tones. Ironically, the message of each mural contradicts the palette used: Adam and Eve are cast out of Eden, and the prophets are predicting salvation through the coming of Christ.

4   AT THE ENTRANCE TO THE WEST transept is a large double pillar bearing dedicatory inscriptions to various Stanford family members. All four pillars holding up the dome have dedications to both Jane's and Leland's immediate families. After the 1989 earthquake, about a third of

THE ORGANS

The church's original organ, built by the Murray M. Harris Co. in 1901, was slightly damaged in the 1906 earthquake. It was disassembled, put in storage, then later repaired and reinstalled in the choir loft. In 1915, an echo organ containing eight ranks of pipes was added in a room built behind a wall of the west transept balcony. The Murray Harris organ was rebuilt in 1925 and expanded in 1933. Thoroughly restored in 1995, the 57-stop organ now has 3,702 pipes, arranged along both sides of the choir loft.

In 1983-84, the second organ, the Fisk-Nanney, was installed in the center of the choir loft. It is named for its builder, Charles B. Fisk, and for Herbert Nanney, University Organist Emeritus.

The Fisk-Nanney is a Baroque-type instrument of 73 ranks and 4,332 pipes. Considered one of the finest organs in the world, it can be switched easily from mean-tone tuning, appropriate for early 17th-century music, to the well-tempered tuning needed for later Baroque music. This is the first instrument in the history of organ

building capable of authentically reproducing nearly all organ music written from the 16th century through the 18th century.

A smaller, third organ, the Potter-Brinegar, is to be installed in the church in fall 1995. This delicate instrument, with its solid walnut case and intricately carved pipe shades, was built by Paul Fritts. It is a mean-tone Renaissance-style instrument with 8 stops and 429 pipes.

The Murray Harris organ is on the right of the organ loft. (Chancel viewed from organ loft)

the area of this transept was converted into a side chapel for the celebration of smaller, more intimate church functions. The altar and chairs were designed and constructed by Bay Area artist Gail Fredell. She used original Salviati mosaics, which had been stored in the basement since the reconstruction of the church after the 1906 earthquake, to create a mosaic band just beneath the top of the altar.

The upper arches of the large windows are highly decorated with small pieces of colored glass, which create an intense jeweled effect. Lamb admired this technique in medieval stained glass and used it here. The glass panels in the lower sections of the windows contain inscriptions. These panels have a marblelike appearance—a green, milky glass streaked with brown that creates a variegated block of color.

Starting from the right, the windows are scenes from the New Testament. *Christ in Gethsemane* and *Christ with Mary and Martha* were designed from original paintings by the German religious illustrator and painter John Heinrich Hofmann. Hofmann's work was also the inspiration for four other windows in the church. He tended to emphasize the theatricality of religious scenes in his paintings. Lamb accentuated this in the first window by the layering of glass and by using the lead lines to intensify the drama. As a result, this is one of the most successful of the figural windows in terms of the manipulation of color and layering of glass, and it shows Lamb at his very best.

The Good Shepherd was inspired by a painting known as *The Door of the Fold* by the English Victorian painter Sibyl C. Parker. Parker was the only female painter whose art work was used in the church.

Christ and Mary Magdalene was taken from the central section of one of Hofmann's paintings. Again, Hofmann created a moment of drama by contrasting the hostility of the crowd with the calmness of Christ.

The window that depicts the miracle of the loaves and fishes is based on the painting *Pan y Peces,* which Bartolomé Esteban Murillo painted for the church attached to the hospital of La Caridad in Seville, Spain.

❧

5 ON THE RIGHT SIDE OF THE CHANcel area, there is a handsome brass lectern designed as an angel holding up a book. This was probably purchased in Europe by Jane Stanford and was dedicated to her deceased husband on the anniversary of his birth in 1902. It was on this date that she had originally hoped to open Stanford Memorial Church.

The three windows behind the altar get direct sunlight most of the day, and there are times when *The Ascension* is truly luminous, with the figure of Christ glowing and dissolving in the sunlight. This window was based on a painting by Johann Karl Loth, a German painter who was known in his adopted city of Venice as Carlotto. It was most probably inspired by Raphael's painting of the transfiguration of Christ, which the window strongly resembles.

This brass lectern was acquired in Europe by Jane Stanford. She dedicated it to her dead husband on the 78th anniversary of his birth in 1902, the date on which she had planned to open the church. The altar rail, seen here beneath the gilded glory of angels, is carved from Carrara marble. (West side of chancel)

The central window, *The Crucifixion*, takes its design from a painting by Ernst Deger. This German artist had a rather romantic medieval view of suffering and death. Many of his paintings were later copied and he had a considerable influence on church art.

The Nativity was based on a painting by the English Victorian artist Edward Fellowes-Prynne. The artist's naïve quality has been adapted well in this interpretation. Interestingly, this artist designed a window for St. Peter's Church in Staines, England, using the same subject.

All of these windows have noticeably thick horizontal support bars. These can be distracting, especially in the gentle scene of *The Nativity*, but it is presumed that Lamb purposely designed these windows with

heavier bars because of the high likelihood of earthquakes.

The mosaics here have a radiant quality. The two panels next to the central window depict angels holding a cross and a crown. This motif perfectly reinforces the subject matter of the central window. Above and beside the windows, there are two tiers of mosaics stretching all around the chancel. The lower tier portrays a glory of angels singing, dancing and playing musical instruments. The tier above this represents a more static group of prophets: John the Baptist, Ezekiel, Samuel, Jeremiah, David, Elijah, Moses and Isaiah. At the top, a number of cherubs peep out.

Directly behind the altar is a faithful reproduction of Cosimo Rosselli's *The Last*

This mosaic, The Last Supper, *is a faithful reproduction of Cosimo Rosselli's original fresco in the Sistine Chapel, Rome. Maurizio Camerino of A. Salviati & Co., the makers of the mosaics, obtained special permission from Pope Leo XIII to copy it. (Chancel, behind altar)*

Supper. It is the most splendid mosaic in the church and was constructed of tiny ¼-inch tiles. The original is a fresco in the Sistine Chapel in Rome. Maurizio Camerino obtained special permission from Pope Leo XIII for Salviati to copy it. The level of craftsmanship is outstanding. The Salviati studio succeeded through painstaking work and careful choice of tonalities in giving the work a three-dimensional quality. The details on the flasks of wine in the foreground, the angel in the distance outside the left window and the devil sitting on Judas's shoulder are astonishing.

The altar, carved by L.M. Avenali from Carrara marble, supports a simple unadorned brass cross that reflects the colors of the mosaics surrounding it. The cross was made by William van Erp of the Dirk van Erp Studios in 1947.

The winged cherubs carved in stone above the golden niches and in the capitals of the pillars are, according to local legend, the faces of children on campus at the time of the construction. The carvings are certainly all different and seem to exhibit distinct personalities.

6 THE WINDOWS IN THE EAST transept are best viewed in the early morning. *The Raising of Jairus's Daughter* was faithfully reproduced from a popular Hofmann painting that was often used in church literature published for young people.

The German artist Anton Dietrich painted the original that inspired the window

This highly polished brass cross reflects details from the mosaic The Last Supper. *The Coman family donated the cross to the church as a memorial to Jane Stanford on Easter Sunday 1948. (Chancel, altar)*

entitled *Christ Calming the Tempest*. Lamb used the lead lines to full advantage to highlight the drama and tension in the composition.

The window *Sermon on the Mount* was based on an original painting by Hofmann. The theme was a favorite of Senator Stanford, who, according to Jane Stanford, "considered it purely divine."

Gustave Doré was a leading influence on the artists who decorated Memorial Church. The engraving used for the window *The Baptism of Christ* can be found at the beginning of the Gospel according to St. John in Doré's 1886 illustrated Bible. With an engraving, the stained glass artist was free to interpret the color.

Christ in the Temple, the last window in this transept, is based on a painting by the Pre-

THE MOSAICS

The mosaics were made in Italy by A. Salviati & Co. of Venice, who hired Antonio Paoletti to design and execute them. They were constructed of small glass tiles, also known as *tesserae*. These were made by two different processes and come in three different sizes. The larger ³⁄₄-inch tiles were used on the higher mosaics. The majority of the mosaics were made from ³⁄₈-inch tiles. The smallest ¹⁄₄-inch tiles were used only for the *The Last Supper* mosaic behind the altar.

The tiles, of colored opaque glass, were made by mixing and melting together several ingredients. The principal one is silica, found in sand. Potassium or sodium salts were used to lower the melting point of the mixture. Oxides of tin were added to render the glass opaque. Tiny amounts of metal oxides were used to color the glass. This syrup-like mixture was poured onto a slab to form ¹⁄₄-inch thick sheets. On cooling, these were cut up into small chunks—tesserae. It is documented that the artisans had more than 20,000 shades of colors available to them.

Gold tiles are the other kind of tesserae found throughout the church. Gold foil was placed over a ¹⁄₄-inch base of transparent colored glass. The foil was then coated with a layer of powdered glass. On heating, the gold was trapped under a layer of protective glass. Salviati & Co. made many refinements to this technique and won wide approval for their work.

This detail from the mosaic Moses Ordered to Take Israel Out of Egypt *shows the fine detail in the leg muscles on the figure of Moses. (West nave)*

Raphaelite William Holman Hunt. The original, which is reproduced on page 54, is now at the City Art Gallery in Birmingham, England. This painting received much public attention when it was first exhibited because it was one of the first paintings to portray Christ with Semitic features. This portrayal and the naturalistic depiction of the figures of Mary and Jesus as mother and son most probably influenced Jane Stanford to choose the theme of the painting for one of the windows.

7   STANDING IN THE AREA DIRECTLY under the dome, in front of the chancel, allows an unrestricted view in all directions. Looking upward, the visitor is presented with an awe-inspiring view of the dome.

It is constructed on a drum—the cylindrical structure with the painted intertwined leafy pattern. The drum rests on the four pendentives—the triangular elements in the corners—which act as the transition between the square plan of the base and the circular plan of the dome proper. Four angels rise out of clouds, one at each corner atop a pillar. Each angel measures approximately 42 feet from wing tip to wing tip and is 16 feet high. These mosaics survived the 1906 earthquake. However, the angel that is looking downward was severely damaged during the 1989 earthquake when an 8-foot section of its left wing fell 70 feet into the crossing below.

The gilded band in the drum above the angels is painted. Jane Stanford had originally intended it to be constructed of mosaic tiles,

The painting Christ in the Temple *(left) by the Pre-Raphaelite painter William Holman Hunt was the inspiration for the stained glass window (right) of the same name. The painting received much public attention when it was exhibited, as it was one of the first to depict Christ with Semitic features. It is now displayed in the City Art Gallery in Birmingham, England. During the Victorian period, it was considered the norm to interpret artists' works in other forms. (East transept)*

but the workmen felt the structure would not support the weight. The Alpha and Omega symbols on the open book represent the Bible. Proceeding clockwise around the dome, the symbols are as follows: The Roman numerals on the two tablets represent the Ten Commandments. The Christmas star represents the Epiphany, when the three kings visited the infant Jesus. The ox represents St. Luke. The dove represents the Holy Spirit. The winged lion represents St. Mark. The chalice and cross/host represent the Communion meal. The lamb is the purifying Lamb of God. The cross encircled by thorns represents the Crucifixion. The eagle (which looks rather like a griffin) represents St. John. The anchor represents Hope, and the angel represents St. Matthew.

The second story of each transept is visible from the crossing. These areas are usually only open for services when maximum seating is required. In the east transept, the fourth figure from the left, the Queen of Sheba, is wearing a belt constructed of "jeweled" or faceted glass. These windows were both designed and created by Lamb, and they are a true representation of his own artistry.

Jane Stanford had what could be described as a Victorian aversion to blank space. A pattern of mosaic figures continues around the upper transept walls. At Jane Stanford's insistence, these were in male/female pairs. In the west transept these figures were, from the right: Helena, James, Margaret, Andrew, Philemon and Thaddeus. The windows are:

The dome, painted with religious symbols, rests on a drum that is decorated with a pattern of painted green vines on a golden background. The dome is framed here by four intricately carved stone arches. The four mosaic angels sit atop the four pillars that support the dome. Close-ups of individual angels are shown on pages 6 and 32. (Dome seen from crossing below)

57

St. Martha, St. Paul, St. Dorcas, St. Luke, Charity, St. Mark, Faith, St. Matthew, St. Ann and St. Simeon. The mosaics are: Elizabeth, Bartholomew, Madeline, Barnabas, Gertrude and Philip.

In the east transept clerestory, the mosaic figures are, from the left: Noah, Noah's wife, Isaac, Rebekah, Jacob, Rachel. The figures in the windows are David, Ruth, Solomon, the Queen of Sheba, Elijah, Esther, Isaiah, Judith, Daniel, Hannah. And the mosaics on the right are: Tobias, Sarah, Nathan, Deborah, Aaron, Naomi. The depth of relief in the carvings here gives a crisp, clear quality to the work on the arches, the balcony rails and the pillars. A team of 10 men spent two years on scaffolding carving the details into these arches and capitals.

This is a detail from the mosaic the Garden of Eden, *which is also seen on page 35. Close inspection illustrates how the tiles were placed to follow the shape of the figures. When viewing the whole mosaic, compare the rich warm colors used here with the cold, pale tones used to represent God. (West transept, door)*

8 THE *GARDEN OF EDEN* MURAL OVER the east transept door is 12 feet by 15 feet. The serpent has tempted Adam and Eve and they cover their nakedness. The abundant garden contrasts with the paler tones used to represent God.

This is the best vantage point to look across at the upper windows and mosaics above the west arcade. (Look at Vantage Point 3 for details.)

The first window along the east wall of the nave, *The Home in Nazareth*, is a charming scene in Joseph's carpenter shop. This is the last of the six windows based on the work of the German artist John Heinrich Hofmann and has an interesting theatrical touch with the young Christ bearing a cross.

The central window, inspired by the

German painter Bernhard Plockhurst, depicts *The Flight into Egypt*. Plockhurst spent his life interpreting biblical events in his art and displayed a religious zeal in most of his works. The three cherubs give the window a particular late Victorian touch. The scene was meant to represent God's guidance to all families as they face the travails of life.

The last window of the series, *The Annunciation*, displays a definite Art Nouveau influence with the sweeping curved lines exhibited in the angel's robes and Mary's pose. Frederick James Shields, a Pre-Raphaelite watercolorist, painted the original *Annunciation* that inspired this window. The decorative nature of the window is consistent with the love of pattern and design displayed in other Art Nouveau works. The flower on the left

THE STAINED GLASS WINDOWS

The genius of Frederick Lamb's work at Stanford is that, for the most part, the original paintings and the finished windows were radically different shapes. The paintings were long, and the windows high and narrow.

It took the J. & R. Lamb Studios three years to make the windows in New York City and eight months to install them at Stanford.

Lamb made initial colored sketches of the window designs so as to work out the proportions and scale. Once approved, these sketches were worked into full-scale drawings. Usually, these drawings were not colored and were used to work out the placement of the lead and the shapes of the individual pieces of glass. Once the glass was cut, the windows were temporarily assembled and set up in bright outdoor light so that the color harmonies could be studied.

The glass was then cleaned, polished and reassembled. The appropriate-sized lead cames (the I-shaped strips of lead that hold together the bits of glass) were fitted and putty was placed be-

tween the lead and the glass to hold the glass firmly in place and to provide a waterproof seal. The cames were then soldered at the joints to form a single coherent window. The lead was very much part of the design and the final visual aesthetic of the finished windows.

Lamb and his contemporaries studied the work of the medieval craftsmen, whom they regarded as the masters of light manipulation. Lamb used multiple layers of glass, known as plating. In some areas, he worked with layered panes, exploiting properties of color, reflection, refraction and transmission. The white pearlescent glass used in much of the clothing —known as drapery glass—is not flat but bent and folded. Some pieces of glass are so various in color that they are small masterpieces in themselves.

The windows at Stanford Church represent the best collection of Lamb windows in existence.

This detail from a stained glass window shows support bars and lead cames. (West stairwell)

and the Holy Spirit on the upper left are all carefully placed to enhance the design. The window, which contains only two figures, works well because of the simplicity of subject matter and the confident manner in which Lamb employed the lighter color tones of glass.

Some of the loveliest of the small mosaic vignettes are placed above the arcade on the main wall of the nave. They are, from the left, *The First Family*, *The Deluge*, *The Tower of Babel* and *Moses Saved from the Waters*. The last is a particularly charming scene.

9 STANDING IN THE CENTRAL AISLE and looking up toward the chancel over the oak pews and up to the redwood ceiling, the visitor can catch a glimpse of the most hidden mosaic in the church. This triangular area in front of the dome hides the mosaic of a child's face. This is the only other mosaic to survive from 1904.

This central aisle is also a perfect place to view the chandeliers. They were placed in the church in 1915 and are in the Art Nouveau tradition, with the decorative patterns cast in pot metal and gilded. Pieces of highly textured blue glass cover the insides of these latticework designs. When the lights are turned on, the effect is reminiscent of the blue enamel and gold filigree designs of medieval jewelry.

There are two mosaics located on the wall between the front doors of the church. Looking from the altar, the one on the left represents Jesus, sitting on a throne with the

The window The Good Shepherd *(left) was inspired by the painting* The Door of the Fold *by Sybil Parker, the only female painter whose art work was used in the church.* Christ and Mary Magdalene *(middle) is a detail from one of John Heinrich Hofmann's paintings.* The Miracle of the Loaves and Fishes *(right) is based on the painting* Pan y Peces *by the Spanish painter Bartholomé Esteban Murillo. After the 1989 earthquake, this west transept was converted into a side chapel, the Lane Chapel, for the celebration of smaller, more intimate, church functions. (West transept seen from nave)*

Book of Life on his lap. The colorful rainbow behind him is a symbol representing God's promise to be merciful to humankind. The other mosaic represents *God the Father Receiving Christ into Paradise*, in which the kings are shown relinquishing their earthly crowns to Christ.

Leaving the church and walking around the exterior, the visitor can see the contrast between the solid, rough-hewn stone walls and the delicate, multicolored windows. From the outside, these windows can be appreciated in reflected light, which highlights the texture in some of the glass panels. In places, the color is very different when viewed from the outside of the church. This indicates the use of multiple layers of different colored glass. By manipulating color in this way, Lamb cre-

ated subtle shades that were not possible with a single pane of colored glass. This helps explain why Lamb was regarded as a master at light manipulation.

Moving back from the façade, the church appears seamlessly integrated into the repetitive arches of the colonnade. Its importance is highlighted by the intricately carved arches that mark the entrance. This feature and the rounded arches and shortened columns are characteristics of the Richardson Romanesque style. Although the architecture is very much in the tradition of Richardson Romanesque, the addition of the decoration suggests the spirit of the American Renaissance style.

Standing at the center of the Quad and looking toward Memorial Church, we are reminded that it is not only the center of the campus but also a place of inspiration. The Stanfords were unyielding in their insistence that the church be the focal point of the campus. As David Starr Jordan, the first president of the University, explained: "The church was to be 13 among 12 buildings about the Quadrangle, thus symbolizing Christ and his apostles and indicating the central place of religion in the thought of the founders and in the life of the University."

On a brilliant California day, with one's eye drawn upward to the Byzantine splendor of the golden mosaic on the façade, it is easy to appreciate why the epigraph *Domus Dei Aula Coeli*—"The house of God, the forecourt of heaven"—inscribed in the vestibule is so appropriate.

This is one of four small mosaics on the façade. This particular mosaic represents Faith. (Façade, between arches)

Jane Stanford wrote to friends from Florence, Italy, on February 25, 1884: *"I have turned for comfort to the giver of both good and evil and my faith has increased, and now again I turn to Him with entreaties to save to me my darling boy."* Jane lost her son Leland Jr. to typhoid fever some two weeks later, but as Memorial Church attests, she never lost her faith.